Fiddle Time Christmas

a stockingful of 32 easy pieces for violin

Kathy and David Blackwell

illustrations by John Eastwood

Welcome to **Fiddle Time Christmas**. You'll find:

- 32 well-known Christmas carols and pieces with words to sing along
- solos and duets using finger patterns 0–1–23–4 and 0–12–3–4
- easy chord symbols for guitar or keyboard accompaniment; these chords are not compatible with the CD performances
- a CD with performances to listen or play along to; the varied accompaniments use piano, guitar, drums, and bass
- piano accompaniments available in a separate volume

Using the CD:
- all carols and pieces are played through twice, except those pieces which include a **D.C.** or **D.S. al Fine**, and 'Hogmanay Reel', which are performed once only
- each carol and piece has a short introduction and a link between the verses
- where there are duet parts, these are mostly added in the second verse
- Tuning track: track 33.

Performers: violin Olivier Bonnici; guitar Pete Vecchietti; double bass/bass guitar Mike Chilcott; percussion/drumkit Jon Buxton; piano David Blackwell. Grateful thanks to Pete Vecchietti for devising the CD arrangements of Nos. 2, 11, 25, and 30.

MUSIC DEPARTMENT

OXFORD
UNIVERSITY PRESS

OXFORD
UNIVERSITY PRESS

Contents

1. Hark! the herald-angels sing
Felix Mendelssohn (1809–47)

Joyfully

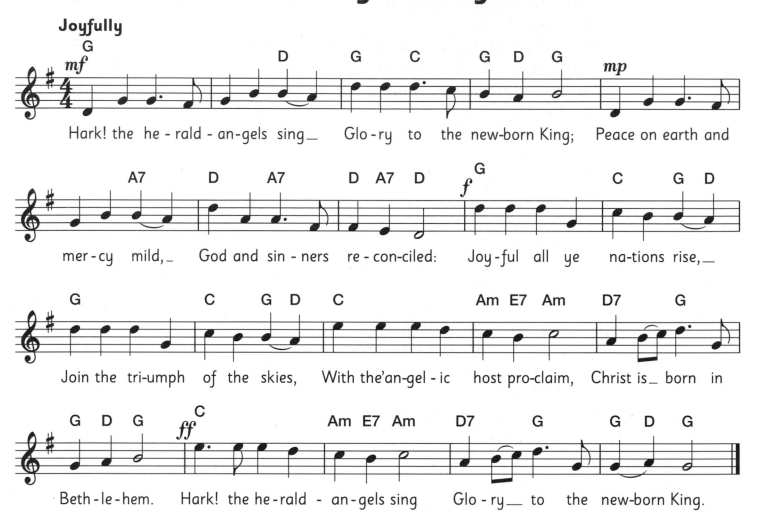

Hark! the he - rald - an-gels sing_ Glo - ry to the new-born King; Peace on earth and

mer - cy mild,_ God and sin - ners re - con-ciled: Joy-ful all ye na-tions rise,_

Join the tri-umph of the skies, With the'an-gel - ic host pro-claim, Christ is_ born in

Beth - le - hem. Hark! the he - rald - an-gels sing Glo - ry_ to the new-born King.

2. Mary had a baby
American trad.

Lively

Ma-ry had a ba - by, Yes, Lord! Ma-ry had a ba - by, Yes, my Lord!

Ma-ry had a ba - by, Yes, Lord! Peo-ple keep a-com-in', and the train done gone!

3. The holly and the ivy

English trad.

Flowing

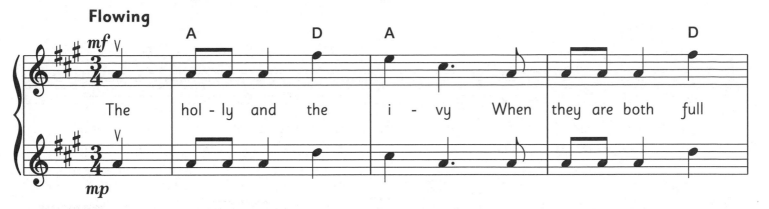

The hol - ly and the i - vy When they are both full

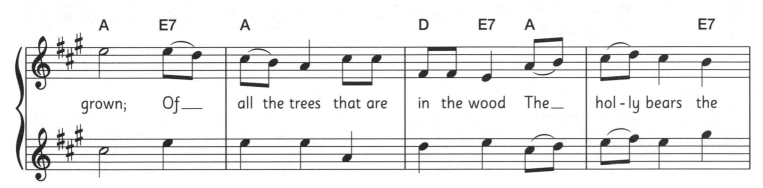

grown; Of__ all the trees that are in the wood The__ hol - ly bears the

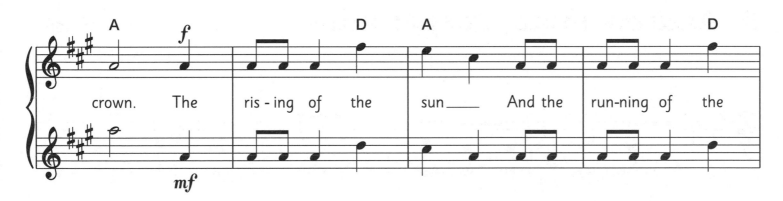

crown. The ris - ing of the sun____ And the run-ning of the

deer, The__ play-ing of the mer-ry or - gan, Sweet sing-ing in the choir.

5

4. Ding dong! merrily on high

16th-century French melody

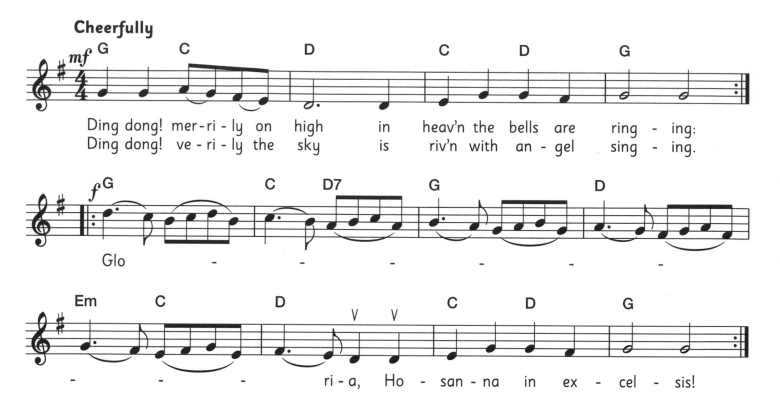

Ding dong! mer-ri-ly on high in heav'n the bells are ring - ing:
Ding dong! ve-ri-ly the sky is riv'n with an - gel sing - ing.

Glo - - - - - - ri - a, Ho - san - na in ex - cel - sis!

5. Andrew mine, Jasper mine

Moravian carol

An - drew mine, Jas - per mine, Ti - mo - thy and A - bel,

Hur - ry to Beth - le - hem, to the com - mon sta - ble.

There you'll find a ba - by small, sleep-ing in a swad-dling shawl;

On your way, on your way, to our Sa-viour born to - day.

Andrew mine, Jasper mine: words by C. K. Offer from *Three Moravian Carols*
© Oxford University Press 1962. Reproduced by permission of Oxford University Press.

6. Silent night

Franz Gruber (1787–1863)

Si - lent night, ho - ly night, All is calm,

all is bright; Round yon vir - gin mo - ther and child.

Ho - ly in - fant so ten - der and mild, Sleep in

hea - ven - ly peace,___ Sleep___ in hea - ven - ly peace.

7. I saw three ships

English trad.

Like a dance

I saw three ships come sail - ing in On Christ-mas Day, on Christ-mas Day, I

saw three ships come sail - ing in On Christ-mas Day in the morn - ing.

8. O little town of Bethlehem

English trad.

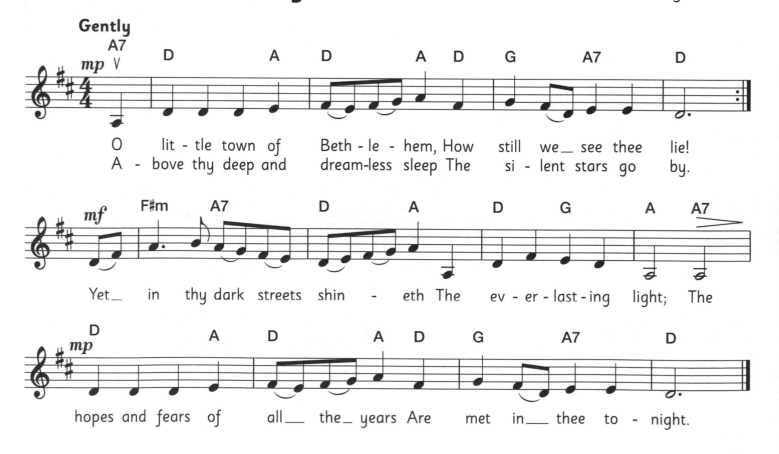

Gently

O lit - tle town of Beth - le - hem, How still we_ see thee lie!
A - bove thy deep and dream-less sleep The si - lent stars go by.

Yet_ in thy dark streets shin - eth The ev - er - last - ing light; The

hopes and fears of all_ the_ years Are met in_ thee to - night.

9. Christmas Calypso

Kathy & David Blackwell

Happily

So dance the Christ-mas Ca-lyp-so in the sun,— Je-sus is born for ev-'ry-one;— Sing out with joy and

Fine

stamp your feet,— move to the ca-lyp-so beat!—

Way back in Beth-le-hem, in a sim-ple sta-ble,

D.%. al Fine

Je-sus, that ba-by boy,— came to save us all! So dance the

10. Once in royal David's city

H. J. Gauntlett (1805–76)

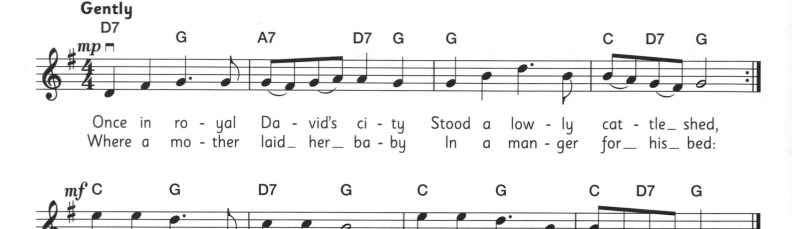

Once in ro - yal Da - vid's ci - ty Stood a low - ly cat - tle_ shed,
Where a mo - ther laid_ her_ ba - by In a man - ger for_ his_ bed:

Ma - ry was that mo - ther mild, Je - sus Christ her lit - tle_ child.

11. Go tell it on the mountain

American trad.

Go tell it on the moun - tain, o - ver the hills and ev - 'ry - where;

Go tell it on the moun - tain that Je - sus Christ is born!

Shep - herds kept their watch - ing o'er wand - 'ring flocks by night; Be -

- hold from out of hea - ven there shone a ho - ly light:____

12. O Christmas tree

German trad.

11

13. We wish you a merry Christmas trad. West Country

We wish you a mer-ry Christ-mas, We wish you a mer-ry Christ-mas, We wish you a mer-ry Christ-mas And a hap-py New Year. Good tid-ings we bring To you and your kin; We wish you a mer-ry Christ-mas And a hap-py New Year.

14. Shepherds watched

Czech carol

Shep-herds watched their lambs and sheep, Through the night so dark and deep. Lo, the an-gel in the skies, Bid-ding them to stand and rise. Hi-dom, hi-dom, hi-do-dom, Hi-dom, hi-dom, hi-do-dom. Hi-dom, hi-dom, hi-do-dom, Hi-dom, hi-dom, hi-do-dom.

15. We three kings

J. H. Hopkins (1820–91)

Stately

We three kings of O - ri - ent are; Bear - ing gifts we

tra - verse a - far Field and foun - tain, moor and moun - tain,

Fol - low - ing yon - der star: O_____ star of won - der,

star of night, Star with roy - al beau - ty bright, West - ward

lead - ing, still pro - ceed - ing, Guide us to thy per - fect light.

16. O come, all ye faithful

J. F. Wade (c.1711–86)

Joyfully

O come, all ye faith-ful, Joy-ful and tri-um-phant, O come ye, O come_ ye to Beth-le-hem; Come and be-hold him Born the King of An-gels: O come, let us a-dore him, O come, let us a-dore him, O come let us a-dore him,_ Christ_ the Lord!

17. Bethl'em lay a-sleeping

Polish carol

Beth-l'em lay a-sleep-ing,

long, so long a-go, | Twink-ling stars were peep-ing, | long, so long a-go,

When to earth a ba-by came the | lit-tle Je-sus was his name, So | long, long a-go.

18. Good King Wenceslas

Piae Cantiones (1582)

Good King Wen-ces-las look'd out On the Feast of Ste-phen,
When the snow lay round a-bout, Deep, and crisp, and ev-en:

Bright-ly shone the moon that night, Though the frost was cru-el,

When a poor man came in sight, Ga-th'ring win-ter fu-el.

19. Deck the hall

Welsh trad.

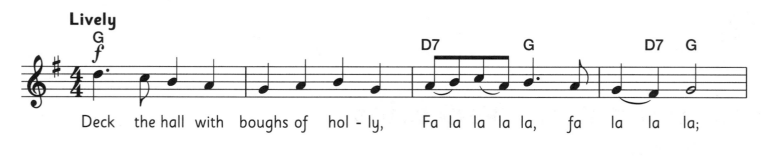

Deck the hall with boughs of hol - ly, Fa la la la la, fa la la la;

'Tis the sea - son to be jol - ly, Fa la la la la, fa la la la.

Fill the mead cup, drain the bar - rel, Fa la la la la la la la la;

Troll the an - cient Christ-mas ca - rol, Fa la la la la, fa la la la.

20. Away in a manger

William J. Kirkpatrick (1838–1921)

A - way in a_ man-ger, no_ crib for a bed, The_ lit - tle Lord
Je - sus laid_ down his sweet head; The stars in the_ bright sky looked
down where he lay, The_ lit - tle Lord Je - sus a - sleep on the hay.

21. The first Nowell

English trad.

The_ first_ No - well the_ an - gel did say Was to cer - tain poor
In_ fields_ where they lay_ keep-ing their sheep, On a cold win-ter's

shep-herds in fields as they lay; No - well,_ No - well, No -
night_ that was_ so deep:

- well, No - well, Born is the King_ of Is - ra - el!

22. Zither Carol

Czech carol

Brightly

Girls and boys, leave your toys, make no noise, Kneel at his crib and wor-ship him.

At thy shrine, child di-vine, we are thine, Our Sa-viour's here.

'Hal-le-lu-jah' the church bells ring, 'Hal-le-lu-jah' the an-gels sing,

'Hal-le-lu-jah' from ev-'ry-thing. All must draw near.

23. God rest you merry, gentlemen

English trad.

On the move

God rest you mer-ry, gen-tle-men, Let no-thing you dis-may, For

Je-sus Christ our Sa-viour Was born up-on this day, To save us all from

Sa-tan's power When we were gone a-stray: O___ ti-dings of com-fort and

joy, com-fort and joy, O___ ti-dings of com-fort and joy.

24. While shepherds watched their flocks

Este's Psalter (1592)

Lively

While shep-herds watched their flocks by night, All seat-ed on the ground, The
an - gel of the Lord came down, And glo - ry shone a - round.

25. Children, go!

Spiritual

Lively

Child - ren, go where I send thee! How shall I
send thee? I'm gon-na send thee one by one, One for the lit-tle bit-ty
ba - by boy, Born, born,_ born in Beth-le - hem.

26. Skaters' Waltz

Emil Waldteufel (1837–1915)

27. Dance of the Reed Pipes

(from the *Nutcracker* ballet)

Pyotr Ilyich Tchaikovsky (1840–93)

28. Jingle, bells

J. Pierpont (1822–93)

Happily

Jin-gle, bells, jin-gle, bells, jin-gle all the way; Oh, what fun it

is to ride in a one-horse o-pen sleigh!__ Jin-gle, bells, jin-gle, bells,

jin-gle all the way; Oh, what fun it is to ride in a one-horse o-pen sleigh!

29. Infant holy, infant lowly

Polish carol

Like a lullaby

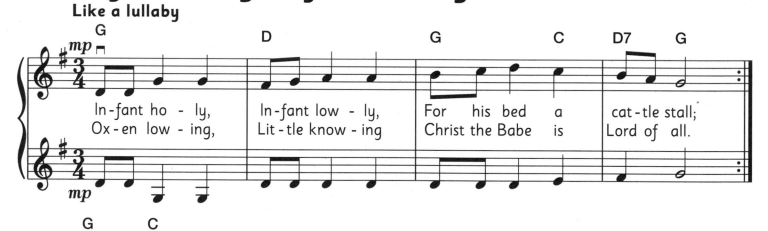

In-fant ho - ly, In-fant low - ly, For his bed a cat-tle stall;
Ox-en low - ing, Lit-tle know-ing Christ the Babe is Lord of all.

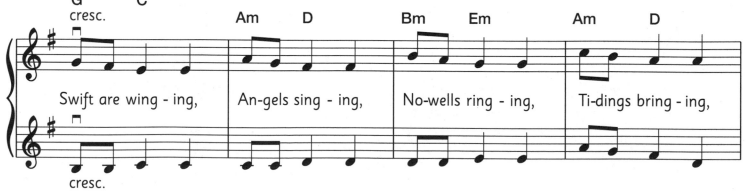

Swift are wing - ing, An-gels sing - ing, No-wells ring - ing, Ti-dings bring - ing,

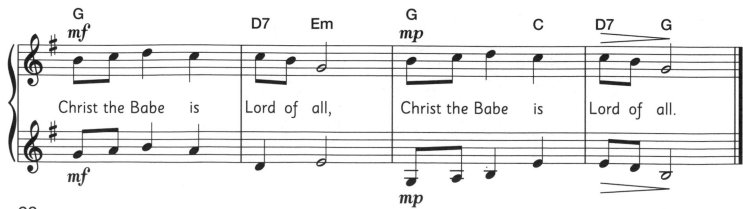

Christ the Babe is Lord of all, Christ the Babe is Lord of all.

30. Child in a manger

Celtic trad.

Gently

Child in a man - ger, Je - sus our Sa - viour,

Born of a vir - gin ho - ly and mild;

Sent from the high - est, Come down in glo - ry;

Tell the glad sto - ry, Wel-come the child.

31. Hogmanay Reel

Kathy & David Blackwell

With energy

32. Auld Lang Syne

Scottish trad.

With a wee dram!

Should auld ac-quain-tance be for-got, and_ nev - er brought to mind? Should

auld ac-quain-tance be for-got, for the sake of auld lang syne? For

auld___ lang___ syne, my dear, for auld___ lang___ syne; We'll

tak' a cup o' kind - ness yet, for the sake of auld lang syne.

24